Up the Watling Street

by Dick Dawson

Bright Pen

A Bright Pen Book

Cover photgraphs:
Dunstable Historical Society (c. 1912)
L Briggs (2012) ©

British Library Cataloguing Publication Data.
A catalogue record for this book is available from the British Library

ISBN 978-0-7552-1522-5

Authors OnLine Ltd
19 The Cinques
Gamlingay, Sandy
Bedfordshire SG19 3NU
England

This book is also available in e-book format, details of which are available at www.authorsonline.co.uk

Blood, violence, and death have plagued the Watling Street since the days when the Romans started building it. The only difference today is that the carnage is caused by motor vehicles.

The road was built over existing grass tracks which were used for livestock and by the local population at the time of the Roman invasion.

The British were made up from a number of tribes and wore animal skins, but their arms and legs were left naked and were usually painted blue, and their hair came down to their shoulders. A lot of time was spent fighting each other and their lives were marked with "cruelty and fierceness."

They had little respect for the elderly and old women could be given away as an inducement for selling grain, and when they became too frail they were thrown out or slaughtered.

The slaves known as "villeins" were almost certainly used by the Romans to help put in the foundations and prepare the Watling Street under the supervision of Imperial troops.

Before that the Romans must have been amazed, when, led by Julius Caesar, they first landed in Britain near Dover and found the rocks and cliffs covered with armed Britons ready to oppose their landing.

But the Britons quarrelled among themselves over who was to be their leader and eventually agreed to surrender. The Romans then discovered that they had occupied a country that was covered in woods and large forests, and inhabited by wild animals such as wolves; and going into these areas was hazardous because if the uncivilised local inhabitants failed to attack you, there was always the danger that you would fall victim to the wild animals. At that time the British lived in wooden houses with a fireplace in the middle, and a hole for letting the smoke out.

There was a high death rate from disease. Tuberculosis and leprosy being particularly prevalent, and there was also a high death rate caused by inter-tribal fighting.

Julius Caesar, who was the leader of the Roman expedition to Britain in 54 AD, and also in 55 AD, was very impressed with the British Belgae tribes' skill in chariot fighting despite their savage ways.

He wrote that they began by driving all over the field and hurling javelins, and the terror they inspired by the horses and noise of the wheels of their chariots was sufficient to throw their opponents' ranks into disorder.

Then after making their way between the troops of the cavalry, they jumped down from the chariots and engaged on foot.

Caesar wrote:" When this happened and were able to control their horses at full gallop and would stand on the yoke and get back into the chariot as quick as lightning."

Caesar said he thought the most civilised of the Britons were those living in Kent and he said they painted themselves with blue woad dye to give a more terrifying appearance in battle.

It was a huge undertaking for the Romans to build the Watling Street, which became the longest road in Britain and stretched from Dover and through London, St Albans, Dunstable, Stony Stratford and on to Hollyhead in North Wales.

Roman engineers built it 24ft across, which was enough to allow two chariots to pass at speed, and they named it after an obscure British tribe called the Waelingi. Today the road is twice that width and juggernaut lorries pass each other at speeds the Romans could never have envisaged.

The Watling Street was very scientifically constructed. First of all the engineers laid a foundation of hard earth that was beaten in. Then they put in large stones, sometimes mixed with mortar, and added various materials such as lime, sand, clay, pounded brick and gravel.

This was far more efficient than the British system of just throwing stones on the road and not compressing them

No expense was spared on construction and the Roman engineers were so skilled that parts of the Watling Street built by them are still in very good condition, particularly those that were covered over.

The building of the road started in a valley near Dover and was designed to run as a terrace at a fairly high level on the Watling side and then went on to Canterbury. At Rochester it ran down the middle of the High Street and then on to London.

Nearly all the road runs in a straight line, and when the Romans came to marshy areas they built it up five feet above the surrounding land which brought the words "High Street" to our language.

They also cleared the forests and woods alongside the route to prevent ambush, because part of the original Roman idea was to awe and scare the primitive British tribes.

But a local woman who was not awe-struck was the warrior Queen Boudicca, who led a revolt in AD 60 during which her army sacked St Albans, Colchester and London and killed thousands of Romans and their British supporters.

Boudicca, who was Queen of the Iceni tribe, from whom the present Icknield Way derives its name, went on to lead her army up the Watling Street to do battle with the Roman general, Sentonious Paulinus, and the result of this was one of the biggest bloodbaths in British history with about 70,000 of Boudicca's army slaughtered, and only 400 Romans killed.

The great mistake made by the British was to bring their families along to witness the battle. They came in carts and wagons and encircled the rear of the British lines forming a significant barrier to movement.

As the armies arrayed for battle Boudicca is said to have told her followers: "Win the battle or perish. That is what I, a woman will do. You men can live in slavery if that is what you want."

Sentonious told his men: "Ignore the racket made by these savages. There are more women than men in their ranks. They are not soldiers - they are not even properly equipped. We have beaten them before and when they see our weapons and feel our spirit they will crack.

"Stick together. Throw the javelins and then press forward with your shields and finish them off with your swords. Forget about booty. Just win and you will have the lot."

In the battle that followed the victorious Romans spared no one and even the British packhorses were speared and added to the piles of bodies.

The red-haired Boudicca, who particularly hated the Romans because they had her flogged, and then raped her two daughters, poisoned herself after a terrible vengeance had been taken by the Roman army on her tribesmen.

As a result of the battle the rebellion ceased and the Romans built a number of forts along the Watling Street, and introduced a service of mounted couriers together with remounting stages with overnight accommodation provided at every second and third stage.

The main objective was to have a road that would give access to a wide area of Britain so that they could deal quickly with uprisings and civil disturbances.

After the building of the Watling Street important crossroads developed in Dunstable where the Watling Street met the Icknield Way and, in terms of road communications, became the centre of England.

The staging posts, which were called Mansios, were generally 12 miles apart and were used to house soldiers who patrolled the areas and protected money in transit. There were also tax collectors who charged a toll on goods, and despatch riders who carried letters and government documents.

Rooms and meals were also available and there were taverns open for thirsty travellers.

In the four centuries that the Romans were in control the Watling Street helped in the development of the area and many Britons became "civilised" and adopted Roman customs.

But quite a lot of the local population lived in poverty and there were so many beggars that the Roman soldiers nicknamed the Watling Street, Via Mendicorum, or "Beggars Way." However the Romans brought peace to the area, and during their time turned the former British town of Verulamium into a thriving modern city.

After they left in AD 410 the country entered the Dark Ages, and a long period of decline set in with bands of Saxons penetrating deep into the English countryside and plundering and murdering all in their path.

Not much is known of what happened in the region for the 150 years after the Romans left, until King Offa of Mercia marched down the Watling Street from his capital near Lichfield and welded Bedfordshire into his empire, and this endured until the Danes sacked Saxon England.

Quite a lot of evidence of the Saxon invasions has been found close to the Watling Street. Including a pit that contained 50 skeletons, which were possibly those of men and women who had died at the hands of the Saxon invaders.

Another discovery was a hoard of Roman silver coins embossed with the head of the Emperor Nero who died in AD45.

Since it was built several valuable hoards and large numbers of British and Roman coins have been found along the Watling Street, including a large copper coin embossed with the head of a king or prince which was found on the old Watling Street. The head is represented with a collar round the neck which was worn by chiefs and leaders of the Ancient Britons, long before the invasion of the Romans.

Also found nearby was a silver coin of Egbert, King of the West Saxons and the first monarch of the Englishmen.

Roman coins found include one with the impression of Titus Flavius Vespasian who was the Roman general who destroyed Jerusalem and was poisoned by his brother Domitian.

Also discovered was a religious trinket called an Ave Maria, believed to have been made in the reign of Offa the Great.

A thick brass coin of the Roman emperor Antonious, dug up from a garden near the Old Priory in Dunstable has the figure of a Roman legionary soldier fully accoutred with his arms, shield and pike.

The same piece of ground yielded a coin of Emperor Antonius Pius, with a representation of one of the pillars erected before milestones were developed.

Many other coins discovered over the years can be seen in local museums.

A range of rooms from various houses in Verulamium have been constructed at the Verulamium Museum at St. Albans and there is also a wealthy courtyard house containing some of the best preserved Roman wall paintings in Britain.

Some other spectacular wall painting depicting imitation columns and panelling can be seen in the wide corridor of an earlier reconstructed house.

The last two buildings represent shops and a theatre that fronted onto the Watling Street, and workshops with the main one occupying the front room, while the back room was used as a kitchen and general living room.

The ceiling is painted with panther's heads and doves and wheat stalks. The panthers were associated with Bacchus, the god of wine and may have been placed by a householder who enjoyed the good life.

In the course of time the Saxons settled down, absorbed the Romano-British culture and accepted Christianity. Some of their words are still with us and these include "bury" meaning a sheltered or fortified place, "Dun" -a hill, " wella" -a spring and "ham" meaning a village or home.

It used to be claimed that the Saxons were cruel and uncivilised, but the discovery of the Saxon Hoard, just off the Watling Street, in July 2009 has given second thoughts.

The hoard, which consists of more than 1,600 items, and is valued at £3.3 million, is the largest collection of Anglo-Saxon gold and silver ever found and was discovered by a man with a metal detector near Lichfield in Staffordshire.

It contains over 1,600 intricate and delicately crafted items of gold and silver including crosses, pommels from swords, pieces of warriors helmets, and strange serpents, which historians say shines a "dazzling light into the shadowy world of the dark ages."

One of the most intriguing finds was a strip of gold inscribed with the Latin words: "Rise up Lord, may your enemies be scattered and those who hate you be driven from your face."

The site of the find is immediately south of Watling Street and only 2.5 miles west of the Roman staging post of Letocetum.

The TV historian, Dan Snow, says the find has the potential to rewrite the history books and there is still much research to be done before the full picture can be revealed.

Without the Roman engineers, Watling Street deteriorated. An eye witness of the time said culverts were washed away and vast lakes developed "on whose shores wayfarers shivered until the floods abated."

The church became alarmed at the problems the unrepaired road was causing and took over the administration at the request of the King.

It paid attention to the poor, and at Dunstable Priory the almoner was instructed to be kind "compassionate, god-fearing discreet and careful" to them.

He was also told he should "look after pilgrims, beggars and lepers that came to his house and to the town and he must also visit the old, lame, bedridden and blind and feed, clothe and comfort those who are sick."

Many of those whom he looked after must have come to him via the Watling Street, and any almoner employed by him had to be suitable to "converse with all manner of guests of both sexes, so he must be well brought up."

He should also be prepared to supply food and drink as required, clean cloths, towels, cups and silver spoons, mattresses, sheets, blankets, pillows, quilts, a clean bowl for washing up and a good fire.

The most important problem facing the monks was lack of finance, and to get round this the church introduced various money-making schemes.

Priests were told that those expected to die shortly should make sure that they had left something for the Watling Street in their will.

Paid-for indulgencies which claimed to get you into heaven were also available, and poor people who wanted to help could present a gift, or do a day's work on the road without payment.

A sign of the general decline of the area was the disappearance of Dunstable which had been a thriving town, but for the next 700 years was nothing but a crossroads.

Before Dunstable came into being, the Roman town of Durocobrivae occupied the site, but it became deserted when marauding Saxons made it unsafe for travellers to go there.

Dunstable was re-established by Henry I in about 1100, to secure the area from robbers who found plenty of cover in the overgrown area where the Icknield Way crosses the Watling Street.

The local author, Laurence Meynell, in his book, 'Bedfordshire', said that no place in Bedfordshire has seen more alarums and excursions in its history than Dunstable, and the reason for this is it was on the Watling Street, which was the great Roman highway from London to the north-west, and marked the crossroads with the Icknield Way

After centuries of stagnation following the departure of the Romans, King Henry's interest in the area started Dunstable off in a big way again, and this was enhanced when in 1132 the King founded the Priory of St Peter at Dunstable, between the Icknield Way and Watling Street and granted a charter which gave the Prior pretty well all the town, together with the market and the school.

The generous nature of the charter led to a series of acrimonious quarrels and disputes between successive Priors of Dunstable, who claimed almost royal powers, and various officials of the King who disliked coming up against a town where their authority was challenged.

In 1170 the martyrdom of a famous figure, Thomas Becket, at Canterbury Cathedral brought prosperity to the Southern section of the Watling Street at Canterbury, which became the country's major centre of pilgrimage.

Becket was murdered in 1170, on the orders of King Henry II who was in conflict with him over the rights and privileges of the church.

Pilgrims flocked to Canterbury after he was made a saint and the monks cashed in, like modern day enterpreneurs, selling pieces of cloth claimed to have been soaked in Becket's blood. It was said if you touched them, you would become cured of diseases and illnesses, including leprosy and blindness.

Visitors could also buy metal tokens with the alms of Canterbury Cathedral embossed upon them.

The massive increase in pilgrims brought much trade and prosperity to the Southern Watling Street, while things were less satisfactory north of London which was suffering from an outbreak of crime and violence.

A town that disappeared after the Romans left was Verulamium, which was founded by a tribal leader called Tasciovanus, who gave it the name Verulamium in about 10 B.C, and minted the country's first coins which bore his name, and also the name of the mint.

It is believed that the words inscribed on these coins are the earliest words written in the English language.

The town, situated west of St Albans was nearly two miles in circumference, and about 200 acres in extent. Round it, defences can be traced, and an earth wall on the Eastern side seems to have been put up to strengthen the defences against siege engines.

The area around it originally consisted mainly of farmsteads but gradually grew into a Romanised city, particularly after the opening of the newly laid-out Watling Street.

But disaster struck in AD 61 when the British Queen Boudicca overwhelmed and sacked Verulamium and killed most of the inhabitants, leaving it a blackened ruin which took 20 years to recover.

Then, building on a large scale took place and the town was surrounded by a defensive wall, and the Romans went on to turn the new Verulamium into the chief city of Roman Britain, with a temple, a town hall and streets on a grid system and with villas decorated with mosaics and a market hall facing the newly laid-out Watling Street.

There was also a triumphant stone arch, built in the second century, that spanned the Watling Street and four gateways with separate entrances for traffic and pedestrians, and a large public lavatory which had wooden seats and water running underneath it and sponges taking the place of toilet paper.

Verulamium prospered and became a market for slaves and servant recruitment, and accommodated many rich people.

After the Romans left Britain in the 4th century there was a decline in prosperity and population and Verulamium went into decline with the theatre being turned into a refuse dump and the temples closed down because they were considered anti-Christian.

The state of decay was such that a large amount of material from the town went towards building the new church on the hill opposite, and the buildings which formed the ancient city were broken up.

There was much civil disturbance and the roads and houses deteriorated and the glory of the past disappeared. The destruction increased when townspeople took hundreds of Verulamium bricks to mend roads and make garden walls.

John of Wallingford, Monk of St Albans, 1221 - 1258
Drawing attributed to Matthew Paris

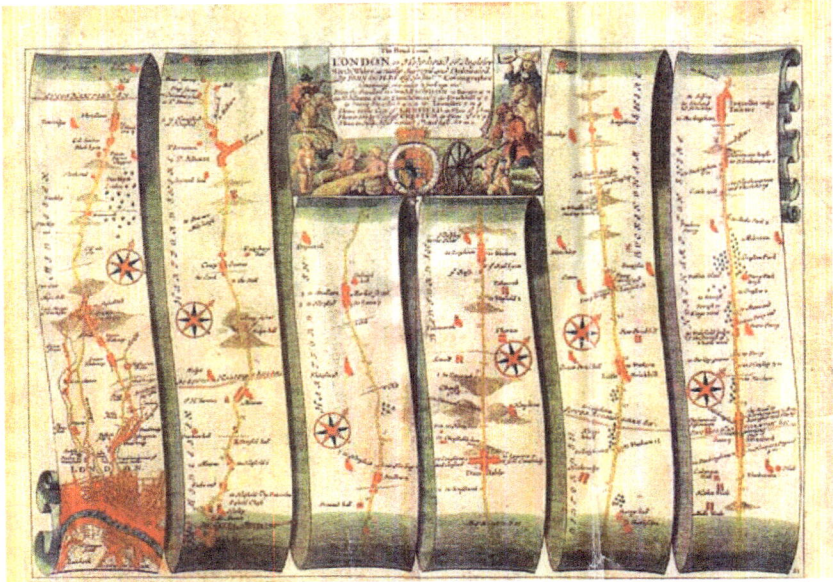

Above: Old map

Below: Roman Verulamium reconstruction

Right: Verulamium Mosaic
depicting the head of a God

Below: Verulamium Mosaic
depicting lion carrying stags head

Antiquarian, William Stukely, who visited the town in 1724 found a good bit of the wall still standing, but said that since then "wretchedly ignorant" people had been pulling it up all round to the very foundations to mend the highway, and he saw hundreds of cart loads of Roman bricks being carried for that purpose when he rode through the old city.

He also noticed the tracks of the old streets were visible when the corn first comes up, or is nearly ripe.

Part of the reason for this declining situation was that Verulamium had become a hiding place for criminals and robbers from the neighbouring forests, and during the tenure of Abbott Ealdred and Abbott Edemer, orders were given to block up all the underground passages in the town because they were the hiding holes of "whores and thieves."

Perhaps, like today, the final blow to local citizens was when the coinage was de-valued and the local inhabitants found themselves incapable of minting new ones. This led to houses falling into disrepair and the town area shrinking in size, with the population going back to subsistence farming and reverting to its pre-Roman state.

Although Verulamium eventually disappeared, it left a splendid legacy in its museum in St Albans which houses one of the best Roman collections in the country.

It was described by author, Roger Wilson. as being "outstanding for both the quality of display and the beauty of the objects which amply demonstrate the taste and elegance of the people of Verulamium."

One of the outstanding exhibits is a mosaic depicting a rugged sea god with beard and claws sprouting from his head.

Also much admired is the Scallop Shell mosaic, laid in about AD 130 which is famous for its subtle and pleasing use of colour.

Another is a dramatic one of a lion making off with the head and antlers of a stag.

A bronze statuette of Venus with a flowing garment round her hips was found in 1959 in a cellar below one of the shops near the theatre.

Other attractions include yellow panels with a scroll design that have been reconstructed. They were discovered when a road was widened in 1955 in the ruins of a collapsed Roman house.

Amazingly, in mediaeval times, two book rolls in Latin, and possibly Celtic, were discovered in a crevice underground in the ruins of Verulanium

They were in perfect condition, but sadly it is not known what they said, because the local monks saw them as the work of the devil and destroyed them.

There is not much other evidence of literacy from the people of Verulamium, although there are some 20 names scratched on dishes and cups, and some beakers were decorated with appropriate mottoes and slogans such as : "Give me strong wine," and some wooden tablets with a surface of wax, were also used for writing.

Contrary to popular belief the Roman toga was not worn in Britain. Instead the Romans wore woollen tunics with short sleeves and a straight slit-like opening on the neck. It was woven in one piece and was loose fitting and never pinned or belted, and was worn by men and women. The women's garments were slightly smaller and were worn over an under-tunic of linen, or fine wool.

Sometimes the men wore capes which came down just below the knee and were fastened with clamps, or thongs.

A lot of jewellery was used, and brooches were worn by both sexes to fasten clothing. Necklaces of glass, or paste beads were common and women's hair was held in place with pins of bone, jet glass and bronze. Finger rings were popular, but only the higher social classes were allowed to wear gold rings. Some rings were set with cut stones and used to seal important documents.

Roman transport, although very slow by modern standards, covered great distances and roads were well built with up to 5ft of gravel in town centres.

Relics of road transport that have been unearthed over the years include "hippo sandals", which were temporary horseshoes, that were strapped, rather than nailed, to the hubs of cart wheels. And there have also been lots of hobnails from the inhabitants boots.

When the inhabitants of Verulamium died they were only allowed to be buried outside the town in cemeteries sited off main roads such as the Watling Street.

Over 1000 burials have been recorded from Verulamium, all dating from AD 1 and 420 and these have provided a wealth of information about the lives of the ordinary people of the Roman town.

The Celts were strong believers in the existence of another world and the dead were cremated along with their clothes and ornaments, and sometimes cherished possessions.

The ashes were then put in a jar and buried together with what the relatives could provide for the journey to the other world, such as food and drinks and sometimes lamps and bells to ward off evil spirits.

A well preserved grave was that of an old man whose ashes were contained in a large glass jar, and laid outside it were the remains of the funeral banquet to see him on his way. Glass counters were found scattered amongst the dishes, which were presumably used for gaming at the feast.

Another notable burial was when the body of a child was found in a lead-lined wooden coffin, which had been placed in a grave lined and covered with tiles. The body had been wrapped in a wooden cloak, and at the foot of the coffin was a wooden box containing green and purple beads and a phallic amulet.

A coin had been placed in the dead child's mouth as a fee to the God Charon, who the Celts believed ferried the dead across the River Styx to the underworld.

The mosaics, and most of the other items mentioned can be seen at the Verulamium Museum, St Michael's, St Albans, AL3 4SW website : www. stalbans.gov.uk

While Verulamium decayed, the Abbey of St Albans had become one of the country's great centres of learning and housed one of the nation's top libraries. There was also a large hall for the monks to entertain visitors and stabling was provided for 300 horses.

As the years went by the efforts of the church in raising money to repair the roads gradually fell away, and there was an increase in the number of criminals who posed as hermits and lived "idle and dissolute" lives on the alms they received for the church.

A local author wrote: "These unlicensed hermits were often peasants or workmen, who had observed how fat and idle a living was obtained by licensed hermits, who had betrayed their trust and fared sumptuously on alms that were unearned.

"The newcomers toasted themselves before roaring fires in their too comfortable cells, and lived in idleness and ease, frequenting ale houses and even worse places."

Eventually the church had a clamp down on them and many were removed or suffered various punishments.

By this time the clergy were trying to cope with a big increase in travellers from the Watling Street and finances were so stretched that there was not enough money to repair the roads and penalties for "foul and dangerous roads" were not enforced.

In the 11th century Leofstam, the Abbot of St Albans, complained that the Watling Street was overgrown and had become the haunt of robbers and outlaws as well as wolves, wild boars and wild bulls.

The most notorious robber was a man called Dunn who terrorised the neighbourhood around Dunstable and gave his name to the town - Dun's stable.

King Henry I made great efforts to get rid of Dunn and challenged him to steal a gold ring and, although soldiers kept watch, the ring was gone in the morning and Dunn got safely away.

Legend has it that Dunn was being chased by a mob and reached the river Ouse where he tore off his clothes and swam down the middle of the stream followed by his would-be captors in boats.

He took refuge on a small island, but his pursuers followed, knocked him down with their oars, captured him and took him to Bedford under strong guard where, without trial, he was led off to be hanged.

The event was the subject of a poem called Dunno's Originals, written by an unknown author, who seems have held him in some admiration which was shared by those who named Dunstable after him.

They used the first syllable to represent his name and the second to represent an underground cave or stable to which he is said to have retreated with his horse in times of difficulty.

Above: Dunn the Robber

DUNNO'S ORIGINALS

Hewn from a rocky spot,
Still by tradition handed down,
The place is not forgot.

Long he defied King Henerie
With all his chosen bands,
And many a Norman proud,
Fell by his ruffian hands.

For many a day they chased him,
When he was on the road,
But dare not follow after Dunn,
Into the Chiltern Wood.

His horse was fleet and strong;
And to the tracts much us'd;
Besides bold Dunn, tho' two to one,
The fight had ne'er refused.

His sword was long, his arm was strong,
He'd been in many a fray;
And in his den, hid from the sun,
The spoil of hundreds lay.

Dunn many winding paths had made,
Which led him through the woods;
Although his chief retreating-place
Was under the cross-roads,

Where oft he heard the soldiers
A cursing of his name;
For comrades that were missing,
Who by his hands were slain.

Long time they watched Dunn,
Unto their pain and cost;
Till they inform'd the King,
Their labour was but lost.

They said he was some evil fiend,
Not man of mortal blood;
But vanish'd in a flash of fire!
When they approached the wood.

Still Henerie resolved was,
To put this robber down;
He said we'll fell this Chiltern Wood.
And here I'll build a Town,

And grant it to my charter !
The Townsmen shall be free!
 But he who kills that Rebel
Sure knighted he shall be !

His armed soldiers felled the woods,
Through fear of Dunn they searched,
And presently discover'd where
His place of ambush lay.

A dreary path o'ergrown with bush,
And roots of lofty trees;

The sight of which amazed them all,
And made their heart's blood freeze

They paus'd a while! but the reward
Again set them to work;
And armour'd soldiers with long spears,
Did guard the passage dark

With flaming torch, and glitering arms,
The cavern they drew near;
But slowly moved with tremblng steps,
Dreading some danger there.

In armour bright their chief advanced,
His Lancers cover'd close;
And great was their surprise to find
Within the cave a horse

Ah sure a noble steed he was,
To ring and staple tied
Who at the sight of men and spears,
Again aloud he neigh'd

Adieu my Dunn! a voice cried out,
From thee I now must flee;
But as for Harry, or his men,
They never shall take me.

They took the horse, in colour like
Unto his master's name;
The King admir'd this noble horse,
He was a horse of fame.

But where's the rebel Dunn, he cried
Have you brought that outlaw?
Oh no, my liege, the chieftain said,
His shade we only saw!

King Henry said, 'Tis wonderful!
That from you he could flee!
But on this spot I'll build a town,
Which Dunstaple shall be.

But first I will try other means
To take this rebel Dunn!
For while he lives I am not safe
Upon the English Throne!

So now prepare a pillar strong
Out of the largest tree;
And from this cave here let it rise,
That travellers may see:

And fix it on Dunn's iron ring,
To which this horse was tied;
Above I'll place my own gold ring,
And there they shall abide

Perchance it may decoy him here,
To steal or cut it down;
But mark ! I prize this golden ring
As equal to my crown!

Instant his orders were obeyed,
The woods with music rung;

These valiant Normans were much pleas'd,
To think they'd routed Dunn.

That daring chief soon heard the news
About this Golden Ring,
He said, We soon will have it down,
In spite of the Norman King.

Dunn marched his gang on that dark night
Unto the Cross road way;
The guards they slew! the Staple drew!
And took the ring away!

Nor could the King with all his men,
This Dunninge ever take;
Until by Houghton witch betray'd!
Was strangled at the Stake.

The staple and the ring they found,
Which Dunn had stole away;
The town still bears them for its Arms
Unto this present day

Long time before Dunn's gloomy cave
Within the Wood was found;
The Roman armies rested here,
Upon this Chiltern ground

And near the present Dunstable
Their station'd Legions lay;
At ancient Magiovimium,
Close by the Icknield Way

After Dunn was hanged the King granted the manor of Flamstead to a knight called, Thurnot, on condition that he and his men guarded the Watling Street and the Western part of the Chilterns and protected the church at St Albans in the event of war.

The Watling Street became a road under the King's protection which meant anyone assaulting a traveller on it could be fined £5 - an immense fortune in those days. The King also ordered that the road should be made wide enough for 16 armed knights to ride abreast.

But despite these heavy penalties and rules, lawlessness continued and the Prior of Dunstable and the burgesses fell out because the townsmen bitterly resented the many privileges the King had given to the church.

Because of this there were riots in 1228 over the payment of taxes and these lasted for the best part of three years in spite of a visit by the King to mediate.

A dispute between the Prior and the townsfolk flared up over the use of the Priory church, with the townsfolk demanding a separate alter for their use and a secular vicar to serve it.

A charter from the King, which favoured the Priors, led to a succession of acrimonious quarrels and the church became extremely unpopular with the townsfolk.

In 1290 an important occasion took place when the corpse of Queen Eleanor, wife of Edward I, was brought down the Watling Street to Dunstable on a bier, which stopped in the middle of the market place and it was decided to use the resting place to put up a memorial cross.

A service was held, and the Prior assisted by sprinkling the ground with holy water. Then the Queen's body, after being laid down, was taken to a number of other towns and villages, and afterwards went on to Westminster Abbey, where she was buried.

A few years later an 'Eleanor Cross' was erected on the Dunstable crossroads to commemorate the event and it provided a spectacular landmark. An eye-witness of the time said it was visible from a great distance and towered above the surrounding houses displaying brilliant reds, blues, gold leaf and gilding on a shiny, bright background.

It remained on the crossroads until it was destroyed by soldiers of the Earl of Essex when they were quartered in Dunstable in 1643.

Further disturbances with the Priory took place in 1371 when the burgesses took advantage of the insurrection led by the populist leader, Jack Cade, to wrest a charter of liberties from the Prior, only to have them revoked after the King had crushed the rebellion.

The rioting spread throughout the whole district and in 1381 Watt Tyler, one of the leaders of the uprising warned the Abbott that he would bring 2000 men to shave the heads of the monks if he reneged on promises of reform. But this failed to come about after the King's army entered Dunstable to crush the rebellion.

The disputes went on until the Reformation in the 16th century which put an end to all the Prior's privileges, and normal jurisdiction prevailed.

John Ball, another revolutionary thought that nothing would ever go well in England until goods were held in common, and as long as there were still gentlemen and villains.

Because of these views he was hung, drawn and quartered in 1381, and after his death the four quarters of his body were rushed up the Watling Street to St Albans to be exhibited in other towns as a warning to others.

The King's comment to his subjects on the events was: "Serfs you were, and serfs you will remain."

At this time there were so many people using the Watling Street, that a family called Malherbes founded the hospital of St John the Baptist at Hockliffe, which was intended for the destitute poor, and was run by a warden and a number of brethren.

Disaster struck when the hospital was burnt down. It was rebuilt after massive fund raising which involved the church handing out indulgences for the remission of sins in return for pious donations.

Later it was taken over by Dunstable Priory, and was put to other uses at the dissolution of the monasteries in the 16th century. Today all that remains is a 15th century, pointed blocked doorway and part of a stone wall.

Because of the hospital, houses were built around it and other dwellings were established in previously uninhabited locations along the Hockliffe stretch of the road.

Another hospital was built on the present site of the Heritage Centre in Dunstable and it still contains the original 13th century fan vaulted stone of the Dunstable Priory Hospitium, which is where pilgrims travelling along the Watling Street and the Icknield Way would have stayed.

In St Albans there were three hospitals, two of which specialised in leprosy.

Little is known of the Leper Hospital of St Julian, founded by Geoffrey de Gorham, 16th Abbot of St Albans, on a spot close to St Stephen's church, and there is nothing to indicate what it may have been like.

The second hospital of St Mary de Pre, was for women lepers and was founded by, Warren de Cambridge, the 20th Abbot of St Albans.

It was situated on both sides of the Watling Street and some of the graves in the churchyard attached to the hospital were visible as recently as 1849.

The hospital was founded after a saint called St Amphibalus who was said to have appeared to a man and said the place where his own bones rested should be sacred and the spot should be venerated.

The Abbot investigated further and learned that St Alban had once appeared in a vision to a layman and revealed the spot where the bones of St Amphibalus rest.

The bones were moved to St Albans, where the shrine of St Alban had been carried out to meet them. Miraculously, it was claimed, the relics had diminished in weight, whereby facilitating the journey.

At the time there was a serious drought, and while the journey was taking place there was a surprise shower of rain which was said to have fallen upon the golden hoods and costly feather work of the monks without wetting them.

The third hospital, Sopwell Nunnery fell into disuse and decay in the days of Charles II. The nunnery became known as Sopwell because of the habit of two devout women, who lived in a hut nearby, of dipping their bread in a spring situated there.

Dame Juliana Berners, who was prioress of Sopwell, achieved some fame because she was the first person to write a book on angling. It was said she was energetic and had something of a masculine character.

Besides fishing she also wrote on the subjects of hunting, hawking and armour. On hawking, she wrote the birds should always be treated gently and owners should be able to understand their sicknesses and weaknesses and should know hawking words of instruction.

Despite the hospitals there was still a great sickness problem caused by travellers passing through and spreading diseases including many coming from the Watling Street.

Infected sick often ended up in one or other of the two pest houses, where conditions were said to be appalling.

By the mid 13th century understanding of ill health and its treatment was improving, and one of the leading doctors of the day, Dr John of Gaddesden, was highly esteemed and wrote a book called 'Modern Medicine.'

Some of his ideas and herbal remedies are still used today but others were unlikely to have any medicinal benefit.

Above: Sopwell Nunnery Ruins St Albans

He understood that tuberculosis led to severe damage of the lungs and could not be treated, and he advised patients in the early stages to prevent coughing by using soothing drinks and ointment, and to have plenty of rest which treatment was perfectly acceptable.

Not so suitable was his treatment of epilepsy by consuming the powdered body of a dead cuckoo, and curing toothache by making the sign of the cross and praying to St Philip.

Dr John had to deal with large numbers of people who had become ill on the Watling Street, including many who had fallen off their horses, and others who had been attacked by robbers and highwaymen.

He wrote a book of advice for travellers advising them to always bathe their feet in cold water, in which herbs had been boiled.

He said if very cold on arrival, do not rush to the fire, but rub limbs, and warm up gradually and before setting out on your travels the next morning, wash the feet in hot salt water and then rub in animal fat.

The doctor advised travellers to always have a good breakfast of roast meat and garlic, with a good wine, and said if the air was "hot and smelly inhale camphor, musk, roses or herbs". And if the air is very offensive hold your nose while sipping wine. A final warning was to wear a hat to avoid sunstroke.

The Watling Street saw more blood and violence during the .Wars of the Roses, in 1461, when war broke out between the Lancastrians and the Yorkists.

The wars were so named because each of the houses used a rose for the emblem of its support.

In the first bloody encounter at the Battle of St Albans, Yorkists and Lancastrians surged round the nunnery at Sopwell in May 1455, and the White Rose triumphed after a short struggle, and Henry VI was wounded in the neck by an arrow and taken prisoner in a shop at St Albans, and from there removed to the Tower of London.

Another battle took place on Bernard's Heath near St Peter's church in 1461 when the Yorkists were driven back towards the centre of the town and then fled when night came.

The Lancastrians plundered the town and the abbey and this so disgusted the Lancastrian-supporting abbot that he changed from being a Lancastrian supporter to a Yorkist.

The Wars of the Roses finally came to an end when Richard III was dethroned by Henry Tudor in 1485.

The Watling Street saw war again in the 17th century when it was used as a supply line by both the Parliamentary and the Royalist forces.

The Parliamentarians under the Earl of Essex moved an army of 8000 men into Great Brickhill. They were opposed by the Royalist forces under Prince Rupert, who was based at Stony Stratford.

Essex's forces were half starved and their morale was extremely low, but it improved when the Royalists failed to attack them and they regained their efficiency as a fighting force.

The following year the Royalists under the Duke of Cleveland took Little Brickhill, and a party of them went down the Watling Street to Dunstable, where they shot the church minister and killed the landlord of the Red Lion who refused to supply them with horses.

During the Reformation, the Priory, which ran the area of the Watling Street around Dunstable was dissolved, and surrendered its property into the Kings hands in 1539, and at the same time the lordship over the town by the last Prior of Dunstable Gervas Markham, came to an end. He was given a pension £60 per annum and died in 1561

In St Albans, the Abbot, who was a loyal supporter of the Parliamentarians surrendered the Abbey in 1539, and for this was given a yearly pension and his monks were given allowances.

The monastic buildings, which covered the hill on the south side of the church in St Albans, were granted to Sir Richard Lee in 1540, who destroyed them, and the rich possessions of the monastery were dispersed among the interested courtiers who had favoured the King.

This led to a scene of "desolation and desecration" and plundering took place, causing much magnificent architectural work to be lost forever, and resulted in the monastic buildings in St Albans "disappearing more completely than those around any other great English monastery."

But in the midst of all the chaos the Watling Street was undamaged and continued to be in service.

When the Cromwellian government became established, many royalists became highwaymen. One of the most notorious was a man called Hinds, who held the dubious record of carrying out 40 robberies in two hours, near Barnet.

Also notorious was James Witney, a former innkeeper, with a 30 strong-gang, who would sometimes ride openly through the towns to the fear of the inhabitants.

He was finally caught at Barnet on the Watling Street after killing a soldier and wounding several others, and was executed.

Another robbery was of £1,500 in cash being carried for the King. The robbers overcame the guards, and killed their horses to hinder t pursuit.

A highway robbery which must have generated a lot of gossip took place in 1772, when the vicar of Hockliffe, Dr Dodd, was proceeding from his home when he was stopped by a highwayman, who discharged a pistol into his carriage, but only broke the windows.

The highwayman was captured and hanged after Dr Dodd had given evidence against him in court.

But in 1777, Dr Dodd suffered the same fate when he got into debt and tried to obtain £4,200 by forging a bond.

There was a petition pleading to the court to show him mercy and not hang him. and the famous diarist, Dr Johnson, wrote a letter to him in prison before his execution which was said to have been one of the most moving things the great man ever wrote.

Further down the Watling Street there was a lot of crime in Highgate area where footpads armed with pitch-plasters attacked people from behind and clapped the plasters over their mouths reducing them to an "enforced silence" which enabled the footpads to empty the victim's pockets at leisure.

Barnet was well known for being the worst area for robberies on the first stage from London. It also had the reputation that because of its convenient distance from London and favourable situation, it was the ideal place for "amorous excursions."

One newspaper report told of an incident where "a gang of ruffians" infested the neighbourhood of Barnet and committed the most daring daylight robberies which had thrown the inhabitants into the 'utmost consternation.'

Sometimes the victims struck back at the highwaymen, and there was much praise for a Dunstable baker called William Kilby, who was returning to Dunstable from St Albans in his pony and trap, and had reached that part of the Watling Street notorious as a hide-out for highwaymen and robbers in the Markyate area.

Mr Kilby always carried a large carving knife in the trap and when a highwayman leapt out of the bushes, he slashed at the man's hand with his knife and the man fell off the cart screaming.

The next day four fingers were found inside the trap when it was being cleaned. The government offered a reward to anyone who could give information leading to the conviction of highwaymen, and this came with a certificate to exempt the informer from certain parish duties.

Meanwhile Dunstable had become a Puritan stronghold and its population had rapidly declined. One of the reasons for this was the continual outbreaks of the plague, which was spread by travellers coming up the Watling Street from London carrying the infection with them.

One of the worst outbreaks of the plague, or Black Death, had taken place in the 14th Century when half the monks at Dunstable Priory, and the Prior, died when they got infected through treating plague victims.

In 1570 the population of Dunstable was about 1,000 and by 1642 it had fallen to about 840. During this time the Watling Street had become a major thoroughfare for driving herds of cattle to the London markets from North Wales and northern England, and Hockliffe was used as an important overnight stopping place with grazing grounds and an increased amount of accommodation for drovers and travellers.

By the 17th century that part of the Watling Street that passed through Dunstable had become North Street and South Street with four streets "pointing to the four corners of the heavens."

In all of the streets mentioned there was a public pond supplied by rain water, and at the entrance to Dunstable, Watling Street became High Street.

On many days over 1000 cattle and sheep passed through the village on their way to Smithfield market, and at Hockliffe there were three yards for shoeing cattle and sheep to prevent them going lame on their journey.It involved nailing flat pieces of metal to their hooves.

Many of the travellers died from sickness, or being assaulted, including large numbers of Welsh men and boys who were driving livestock from Wales to the London markets and died along the way.

Some traffic rules were introduced, including the use of partly covered wagons with broad wheels, because it was thought that these acted as a kind of roller, while narrow wheels were a nuisance because they made deep ruts.

There were special rules for traffic using part of the Watling Street at Puddle Hill, near Hockliffe, which stated loaded wagons could be drawn up the hill, provided that their wheels were nine inches broad, and that they were pulled by up-to-ten horses.

Wagons with narrower wheels were not allowed more than six horses which meant they could only take light loads.

After they passed through Hockliffe the coaches then had to leave the straight line of the Watling Street and bear round to the right below the hamlet of Chalk Hill, and then come back to the highway just below Houghton Turn because the road was so steep.

Before that when the Watling Street was still being used coaches were dragged over Chalk Hill with the aid of four extra horses.

The new cutting around Chalk Hill was finished in 1838, and cost £10,000. The cutting was carried out in sections until one half of it had been lowered, and then this narrow road was used by the coach drivers while the navies were cutting away the remainder.

The contractor, called Jackson finished the job in two years, with the help of 40 horses, a gang of navvies and three-wheeled rail trucks called "dobbins." As the chalk was cut out of the hill, "dobbins" transported it to a resting place up the road below the village.

The work of the horses was mainly to bring back the empty dobbins which were run down by natural gravity to the place of emptying, but some of them were also used to cart material to help build the Sewell Road.

Highway robberies were so frequent in this area that an arch, called Gib Arch, was put up in a field just below Hockliffe.

It is believed the last person to be put on the gibbet was a native of Sewell, near Dunstable, who was sentenced to death for attacking and robbing a mail coach between Dunstable and Chalk Hill.

Another mail-coach robbery took place when the Chester Mail was robbed by three highwaymen who carried off all the letters out of 41 boxes.

A reward of £200 was offered each, for apprehending he highway men upon conviction. There was also a reward given through an act of Parliament.

Two brothers named William and Thomas Bibbie were captured and detained in Newgate prison, but William met his death when he escaped from the prison and then died from injuries sustained when he was clambering over a fence during the escape.

His brother was convicted on a charge of robbing the Chester Mail in the company of his brother, and was hanged in chains near St Albans.

Despite all the robberies and crimes going on in their area most of the local farmers continued to provide hay and grain for the passing herds of cattle and sheep and there were large numbers of "muckles", or manure heaps in the village, but unfortunately for the locals this lucrative trade declined when the railways arrived and towns and villages on the Watling Street became impoverished.

Nearby, Little Brickhill had also benefited from the increased trade coming from the Watling Street, and an army of ostlers, stable boys, shoeing smiths, wheelwrights and coach repairers moved in just as they did at Hockliffe.

By now ladies could order two seats and travel quite safely across the country with their maid or servant.

There were 13 inns and pubs altogether in the village with the large inns being used by the upper classes, while less well off people and the servants went to the smaller ones.

The mail coaches, which changed horses after every 12-15 miles and provided overnight stops, enabled travellers to stable their horses at an inn in one of the two villages and then wait for the coach.

At Redbourn there were five inns and the droppings of the coach horses provided a precarious living for a widow called Mary Lofty who started picking up horse manure because she could not think of any other source of income. She would get up at 3am to get the first load which she put into an old wrapper and would work right through to late at night for the last coach. She sold the horse manure to farmers for a pittance, but eventually made enough money to buy an old box which she strapped round her waist and used for carrying the manure. The villagers were so impressed by her hard work that they clubbed together and bought her a wheelbarrow.

The way Hockliffe depended on Watling Street traffic can be seen in this register of local businesses.

Richard Abless -blacksmith; Joseph Chase -sadler; George Cook -landlord, Fleur de Lis; John Green -landlord,White Hart (and cattle salesman); John Heckford - landlord, White Horse Inn; William Inwards -landlord , White Horse (and butcher); Henry North -ginger beer manufacturer; George Roberts -wheelwright; William Torrington -blacksmith; Michael Woods - landlord, White Swan.

Then the slump in passing trade caused by the arrival of the railways led to a decline in prosperity along the whole Watling Street.

Most of the inns were sold to house buyers and many people left the villages, while John Morris the last tenant of the White Hart at Hockliffe, hanged himself.

Before that the village had been totally enclosed and there was antagonism because enclosure led to the end of common rights.

But it was argued that when they lay open before the enclosure, the fields were spoiled and trodden with cattle, sheep, pack horses and hackneys, because of their nearness to the Watling Street.

When the old tracks developed deep ruts, or where mud had rendered them impassable traffic had to go round to the nearest firm spots.

A traveller commented: "Such sprawling and straggling of coaches and carts utterly confound the road in all wide places, so that it is not only un-pleasurable, but extremely perplexing and cumbersome both to themselves and all horse travellers."

These pickings and choosings occasioned many disputes between the packhorse men, who carried goods slung across their horses' backs from one part of the country to the other, and between the market folk and those who travelled on horseback and coaches.

Many of the arguments were over who should take the clean, and who the muddy part of the road. When there was a lot of traffic hundreds of pack horses, wagons and coaches fought and schemed for precedence. It led to many travellers having to stand behind their conveyances and having to wait for hours.

Besides the pack horsemen there were a large number of pedlars, packmen, hawkers and travelling performers and hundreds of tramps.

There were also knife grinders who had contraptions that could be wheeled about the streets like a barrow, and you sat on it in order to treadle the wheel to grind the knives.

Allied to the pedlars were the chapmen, some of whom sold cotton goods carried in horse packs from Lancashire and Yorkshire; and petty chapmen who sold rabbit skins and cheaper goods.

The packmen also carried their goods on a pack-horse, or mule, and would sell goods like cutlery and textiles which they bought in districts where these were manufactured.

There were also a limited number of hawkers who cried their wares in the streets, and hucksters who were similar to the pedlars and hawkers, but used a booth, or stall, to sell their wares.

A tranter was a hawker with a horse and cart who did carrying jobs as well, and many of them traded along the Watling Street.

Another category was a "badger," who dealt in corn, fish butter and cheese, generally using a donkey with panniers for transport."

Higglers were itinerant dealers who carried their wares by horse and cart and dealt in poultry and dairy produce and sometimes in coal, rags and bones.

Rags and bones were also sold by traders who often used old prams to convey them.

Another familiar character was the 'Stop-me-and-buy-one,' ice cream seller who pedalled a tricycle carrying a refrigerated box for the ice creams.

There were also people around who sold food, including sprats and herrings, which had come up from London and were hawked on the streets.

On fair days, nuts were sold at 2d a pint and there was a fried sausage stall which youngsters called 'worm hangers.'

Entertainment was provided by clowns who amused the crowds with antics and buffoonery. And if you had an unwanted cat there was a man who would drown it for you for 6d.

By now many famous people were travelling by coach along the Watling Street and a lot of them liked to hold the reins and be the driver.

They included the Dukes of York, Gloucester and Clarence, and Lord Byron the poet, and Dan O'Connor, the Irish nationalistleader.

The liveliest was the Marquis of Waterford "who would travel up and leap over the hedges in his spring heeled boots, to frighten good law abiding people out of their wits."

The original name of Hockliffe - Hockley in the Hole -was given because of the appalling state of the road which had a national reputation for bad conditions, but in 1724, Daniel Defoe,the author of Robinson Crusoe wrote of it :" We now see the most dismal piece of ground for travelling that ever was in England handsomely repaired from the top of chalky hill beyond Dunstable and through Hockley, justly called Hockley in the hole."

Coaches going through Hockliffe included the bright yellow Northampton coach which was called the "Yellow Wonder". Others included the Tally Ho Express, The Independent and the Power of the Peak. The Holyhead Mail carried a coachman and guard dressed in scarlet uniforms and the guard was armed with a blunderbuss in case of highwaymen.

At the White Horse pub at Hockliffe, local author Charles Kilby said the horses drew up "all of a lather" and boys would come running out with fresh horses, and the porter that rode at the side of the coach would shout out to passengers: 'Box Sir?' Or: ' You sit in the front, sir.'

Then the coachman would come up and have a joke with some of the nearest passengers, and he would mount the box and take, up the reins telling the passengers to "hold hard".

Poorer people travelled in wagons which were much cheaper than stagecoaches. The wagons carried goods, and had teams of eight to ten horses which travelled 20 miles at 3mph before a change of horses was needed.

When the change took place the incoming coachman blew a bugle, a mile or two before reaching the destination, and the new team would be prepared for immediate change over.

Regularly on the Watling Street there were carts conveying vagrants back to their place of origin ,and another common sight was groups of manacled prisoners being taken to London by the County Jailer.

The charge was 6d a mile for a cart, 3d for a horse, and the claimant had to swear on oath that he would not carry any vagrants. If there were only one or two passengers, they rode pillion, but if there were several a wagon was used, and at night a man had to be paid to guard the prisoners.

Other means of travelling, besides carts and coaches, were Sedan chairs , which were used to transport a seated passenger carried by two chair men and often these got stuck in the mud in wet weather and were liable to accidents .

Many inns would hire out horses to travellers. Often journeys took much longer than expected and a trip from London to Cornwall could take as much as six days, while one from Perth to London could take two or three weeks. A few people walked but this was not popular and was scorned by a lot of people. A German visitor called Heinrich Bretschneider, and a companion, decided to walk from London to Liverpool despite being warned about the popular prejudice against pedestrians. On their first stop they asked a woman for a glass of water and she curtly refused saying it was ungenteel to drink water when there was wine, beer and cider available at the nearby inn.

They went off to try and get a bed for the night and were turned down by numerous inns until they reached one where the landlord was Irish and his wife was French. They were disliked by their neighbours as foreigners and Papists. This meant they did not have the English prejudices, and were pleased to give their new guests a bed for the night.

Like today's wind pumps, windmills in those days led to a lot of ill feeling because they frightened the horses and could cause accidents.

James Bell, a Hockliffe farmer, was ordered to remove his windmill on the Hockliffe road because of public complaints. He unsuccessfully contended that he had nowhere to re-locate it and this would mean he would have to sell it at a loss.

Poaching was a big local industry in the Hockliffe area, particularly deer from the Woburn estate, and some poachers used to meet coaches at night to offload their stolen venison.

At Christmas time the coaches would be heavily laden with passengers with geese and hampers swinging from the sides.

One of those who was grateful for the Watling Street, was a man called Hine, who had trained his horse to go lame whenever a stranger got on it. He would then sell the horse to him and pocket the money. When the buyer got on the animal and it went lame, Hine "feigned astonishment" and asked to be allowed to mount it to see what was wrong.

No sooner had he done this, when he plunged both spurs into the horse and quickly vanished from the scene waving a polite waving farewell as he left.

At this time the Watling Street was a breeding ground for crime of all kind, and a feature of many parts of the country were gallows by the side of the road.

At Fenny Stratford the gallows were at the junction of Woburn Road and Sandy Lane, and in 1562 ten men were hanged there on one day and a woman called Cecily Revis was burned at the stake. And in 1618 three women were burned there in a single day.

Elsewhere near Dunstable there were gallows at Puddle Hill and another at Thorn Turn.

The Prior of Dunstable had his own gallows for hanging thieves at a place in the town called Edostrode, and there is a field there called "Stretch Field," which is described as "a graphic description of the work of a gibbet there."

A local habit was to leave the bodies rotting on, or by, the gallows, and on one occasion to the great amusement of the locals, a sparrow built a nest in the skull of a man who had been hanged.

At Kate's Hill there was a gibbet on which were hung the bodies of highwaymen, who were tied by chains and fully dressed, and then enclosed in an iron framework which "swung creakily in the wind."

When coaches began to take the place of horsemen the importance of Dunstable increased. The first stagecoach passed through Dunstable in 1742, and sixty years later no fewer than 80 coaches a day rattled through it, many of them changing teams there.

When coaching was at its height, Inns such as the Saracen's Head and Sugar Loaf sprang up and prided themselves on providing a meal in 20 minutes.

They were good eaters at that time, and the 20 minute menu at the Sugar Loaf consisted of a boiled round of beef, a roast loin of pork, a roast aitchbone of beef, and a boiled hand of pork with peas pudding and parsnips, a roast goose; and a boiled leg of mutton.

Travelling by stagecoach was also an excuse for heavy drinking and one passenger recalls how he went into a pub in St Albans and met a wine and spirit salesman called George Rumney.

He said :" Rumney trudged with faltering steps from one inn to the other, and from public house to public house where his principle, if not entire business was transacted drinking porter, or ale with one spirit, and with another, wine.

"Then he ordered a lightly seasoned grill, but could. not eat it." Many of the public houses were very prosperous, and in its hey-day the Sugar Loaf at Dunstable had a stud of greys and 40 pairs of horses of its own for transporting travellers.

Travelling in those days was a hazardous occupation, made worse by coach drivers racing each other. In 1832 The Liverpool Express overturned near Hockliffe during a race, and the horses dragged the coach on its side for some distance before anyone could stop them.

The result was that one old man got his leg caught in the ironwork and when the horses eventually stopped the leg had been mangled off. The driver and the guard were both charged with causing injury.

Another crash took place during a race between the Holyhead Mail and the Chester Mail. One of the passengers wrote: "In a moment two spick-and-span turn-outs full of passengers were more or less alive and alarmed, into a mass of struggling horseflesh and groaning wounded."

Among the passengers, one died as a result of the crash and the two coach drivers were kept in irons in St Albans for six months before being sentenced to 12 months imprisonment in the county jail.

Winter storms were always dreaded by the coach drivers, and in 1826 the Tally Ho and the Holyhead Mail both got snowed-up in the Dunstable cutting, and had to be dug out and have their wheels taken off and carried to the top of the hill.

But the worst snowstorm was on January 25 and 26 1881 when it snowed for 48 hours without stopping.

The Watling Street was closed because of snow drifts which were eight or nine feet high, and traffic on all roads and trains came to a halt.

Farmers who had come to the market were unable to get home and had to find lodgings in pubs and hotels, or stay with friends. Everywhere was jammed up, and weary travellers took up all accommodation with 20 of them moving into the station masters home.

The blockage lasted for four days and several hundred men and boys were employed in shovelling snow and digging out trains.

Among the saddest victims were sheep that died in the storm because the wind accompanied by the snow was so strong that it could blow any weak animal off its feet, and it was chilling enough to "stagnate the life blood."

A graphic picture of what it was like travelling by stagecoach was given by the author , Jeffrey Farnol, who stood by the Watling Street at Little Brickhill and gave this description of the arrival of a stagecoach.

"Then it came at a gallop, rocking and swaying a good fifteen miles an hour, while clear and high rang the cheery notes of the horn.

"And now from the cool shadows of the inn yard, there rose, a prodigious stamping of hoofs, rattling of chains and swearing of oaths, and out came four fresh horses, led by two men, each of whom wore top-boots, a striped waistcoat and chewed upon straws.

"And now the coach swung round the bend and came thundering down with chains jingling, wheels rumbling, horn braying, and with a stamp and ring of hoofs pulled up beside the inn.

"And now what a running to, and a prodigious unbuckling and buckling of straps, while the smiling faced coachman fanned himself with his hat, and swore jovially at the ostlers."

Not so enthusiastic was this extract from Hone's Table-books written in the style of Jingle. One part was about what it was like riding on the outside of the coach, and the other as a passenger inside.

INSIDE

Crammed full of passengers - three fat fusty old men - a young mother and sick child - a cross old maid - a poll parrot - a bag of red herrings - double barrelled gun (which you are afraid it is loaded) - and a snarling lap dog in addition to yourself.

Awake out of a sound nap with the cramp in one leg and the other in a lady's bandbox - pay the damage (four or five shillings) for gallantry's sake.

Getting out at the half-way house and stepping into the return coach - and finding yourself at the very spot you started from the evening before. Not a breath of air - asthmatic old woman and child with the measles - windows closed in consequence - unpleasant smell - shoes filled with warm water - look up and find it is the child - obliged to bear it - shut your eyes and scold the dog - pretend to sleep and pinch the child - mistake - pinch the dog and get bit - Execrate the child in return black looks. Coach off for next stage lose your money - get in - lose your seat - stuck in the middle - get laughed at - lose your temper - turn sulky - and turned over in horse pond.

OUTSIDE

Your eye cut out by the lash of a clumsy coachman's whip -hat blown off into a pond by a sudden gust of wind - seated between two apprehended murderers and a noted sheep stealer in irons - who are being conveyed to jail - a drunken fellow half asleep falls off the coach - and in attempting to save himself drags you along with him into the mud. Coach turned over - one leg under a bale of cotton - the other under the coach - hands in breeches pockets - head in hamper of wine lots of broken bottles versus broken heads. Cut and run - send for surgeon - wounds dressed - take post-chaise - get home - lay down - and laid up.

In those days Little Brickhill teemed with Inns and saw a constant stream of coaches arriving and departing with up to 40 horses changed daily without counting large numbers of private vehicles and wagons.

There had been coaches before 1742 but these were more like lumbering wagons and had no springs and because of the state of the roads they took far longer to get to their destinations. and were described as "a cursed kind of carriage."

The first stagecoach which passed through Dunstable in April 1742 took three days to do the journey from London to Birmingham, and Chalk Hill presented a major difficulty with four extra horses having to be hitched on to pull the coaches up the incline.

These conditions led to the installation of turnpikes which were used to defray the heavy cost of repairing the roads. They required toll gates or bars and toll houses to control the traffic and collect tolls and keep the turnpike roads in a good state of repair.

They also undertook some quite major works such as putting in a new cutting at Chalk Hill.

The main coach stopping and changing places on the Watling Street were St Albans, Dunstable, Little Brickhill and Stony Stratford and the average speed was not much more than in Roman times

The Turnpike Act provided that trustees could create gates or turnpikes on certain roads with average charges being one shilling for a coach, six pence for a wagon, one pence for a horse and one penny for a score of hogs, or a score of sheep or lambs.

Any carts with hay at harvest time were free, and so were troops with prisoners and troops on the march. The turnpikes were very unpopular and those manning them often got beaten up and had their takings stolen.

At the Houghton Regis turnpike, Samuel Widdicombe, was charged with assaulting a toll collector called Ben Knibbs with a horse whip, giving him "terrible wounds and bruises in and about the head, neck and shoulders, arms, back, breast and other parts of the body of which he languished in considerable pain for a great time."

Other travellers widened the axle length to pass the turnpike and then narrowed it afterwards, which meant they could avoid the charge.

Local farmers were expected to supply labour to work on the turnpike roads and they could be fined if the roads were in bad condition.

The section of the road from Stony Stratford to Brickhill was not

Above: Chalk Hill Cutting Dunstable

too bad although there was a steep climb out of Stony Stratford, and another at Little Brickhill.

But the next section through Hockliffe to Dunstable was very difficult until, Telford, the famous road engineer, re-graded and improved it, and also demolished Barnet Hill which had needed extra horses for coaches going up it.

The climb up the face of the Chilterns to Dunstable posed a heavy toll on horse flesh, and there are stories of children running beside the coaches with stones and bricks to "sprag" the wheels when there was a danger of a runback, in order to earn a few pence.

The way the native British people dealt with repairing the roads was to use dirt scraped from ditches and water-courses in which they embedded the first cart load of stones which came to hand.

These stones were of all kinds and sizes with the result that the roads were frequently as bad as ever and constantly in the most rugged condition and the repairs and roads were very inferior compared with Romans times.

Above: Houghton Regis Toll Gate

Things improved when a famous blind road maker, called John Metcalf, adopted faggots as foundations over muddy grounds.

Then Telford and another engineer, the famous Macadam, changed the whole system of road repairs by using a layer of smaller broken granite which was bound together by a sprinkling of red gravel, mixed with clay, and used only small stones that could be stuck together.

This was alright until the motorcars arrived which sucked up the dust between the stones and blew it into the air.

Numerous experiments were tried and it was found that spraying tar on the road surface did the trick - and in this way tarmacadam was invented.

One person who was exempted from paying turnpike charges was Old Lal, described as "a pauper without legs, but of a sporting turn of mind." who liked to drive between Dunstable and Hockliffe

He rode in a little box carriage, with only a board to sit on, which was pulled by three foxhounds. He drove it at great speed and his dog team were well matched in size and cleverly harnessed, so he could dash past stagecoaches " like a shot from a gun."

When Lal was not driving his carriage he spent a lot of time at the Sugar Loaf in Dunstable begging for alms.

His end came when he went out for a drive and never returned. The following day Trojan, the lead hound, appeared on his own in Dunstable with some harness still attached to him.

A search party went out and Old Lal was found dead by the side of the road with his carriage jammed between two trees, and a dead hound at the traces.

Lal's friend, who was a groom at the Sugar Loaf, came to the conclusion that the third dog, called Rocket was probably the culprit, because he was a dog that was very fond of sport, and when he smelt a fox he would run after it. On this occasion it appeared he had gone out of control and eventually crashed into a tree with disastrous results for Old Lal.

Having no legs, Old Lal was buried at Dunstable in a specially prepared square coffin. His only mourners were the groom and the dog, Trojan.

Another local character, who could be seen sometimes on the Watling Street, was an Italian organ grinder called Lorenzo Losi, who became well known because the music he played was so ghastly.

It was said anyone who had seen his extraordinary visage and heard the music that was ground from his organ could not easily forget him.

His organ was a venerable instrument that originally produce popular tunes of 20 years before. One by one, however, the pipes had succumbed to the rigours of an outdoor life leaving only about a dozen still functioning.

Someone who listened to him commented: "When he turned the handle the effect was horrible. The surviving pipes all did their part bravely, but the prodigious gaps, both in the air and the accompaniment, reduced the tone to a series of wild shrieks and groans."

One advantage of Lorenzo's musical efforts was that people would give him a copper or two on condition he went out of earshot. Another thing about him was that it always seemed to rain when he was around and this got him the nickname of "Wet Weather."

Huge loads being transported down the Watling Street have long been a common occurrence, and army tanks that went along it during the last war caused damage to the surface.

But the most nightmarish journey of all involved the biggest bell in England being transported from Leicester to St Pauls Cathedral in London in 1881. Known as "Great Paul" the bell, which is now lodged in the south-west tower of the cathedral, weighs over 16 tons, has a diameter of 9ft 6in. and sounds the note E-flat.

When it was made ready for its journey the whole bell and trolley with the launch platform for unloading, weighed 22 tons.

It had been hoped originally that Great Paul would be taken to London by rail, but the railway companies refused to take on the job because of the weight and the danger of it causing a derailment.

So instead it was decided to transport it by road with two traction engines. Things went reasonably well until it got to Little Brickhill

Below: Italian Organ Grinder

Above: Big Paul The 22 ton church bell that blocked the Watling Street

where the road kept giving way, and this problem continued all the way to London, including a particularly long stop outside the Bell at Hockliffe.

Another big vehicle was the country's first steam carriage that carried passengers along the Watling Street in the middle of the 19th century. It weighed about two tons and travelled at 10 mph with the driver sitting in the front and steering with a lever rod.

The tank which contained about 60 gallons of water, was placed under the body of the coach and ran its full length and breadth, and as coke was used for fuel there was no smoke.

The arrival of the steam carriage, which was developed by an inventor called Goldsworthy Gurney, was greeted with great anger by the stagecoach owners, who first of all tried to get them off the road because they frightened the horses, and when that did not work they managed to get road tax on steam carriages increased so much in 1871, that they were put out of business. It could have been a major scheme because the steam carriages charged much lower fees than the stagecoaches, which was probably the main cause of the stagecoach owners' grievance.

The problem of lawlessness continued to be a serious worry and the death penalty was sometimes given for minor offences such as sheep stealing and for any theft of money of more than a shilling.

There were also long periods of imprisonment, sometimes up to seven years, for the theft of property and a lot of people were sentenced to be whipped or placed in the stocks, and others to be transported abroad to places like Australia.

Not everyone was hanged for murder. The rather ambiguous rule was a man who had been "overtaken by a nasty temper," or "had sympathy," was allowed to take refuge in the local church and could remain there for 40 days.

Below: The Watling Street Steam Carriage 1860

Or, in the presence of a coroner, he could promise to leave the country and go in sackcloth and carrying a wooden cross to a port indicated by the coroner, where he was to take ship abroad.

You could also escape a capital sentence and be branded instead, by pleading "benefit of clergy" which involved reading what was called the "neck verse", which demonstrated your ability to read.

In 1677 a man called John Bubb was reprieved from a death sentence for manslaughter after sending in a petition which said: "I have suffered enough misery as so doleful place could be capable to inflict and am likely to perish."

Traffic offences in those days were enforced fairly rigorously often with heavy fines for speeding. Local people could be charged with not maintaining their roads, as was the case of the village of Battlesden when all the inhabitants were charged with not maintaining the highway between Hockliffe and Potsgrove, but the sentence was quashed for "insufficiency."

In general the state seemed just as interfering as it is now, with all sorts of rules and regulations and customs officers keeping watch in every town.

On the Watling Street there was a case where William Rhodes, of Hockliffe, was charged with recklessly driving a wagonette with broad wheels drawn by eight horses, down the Watling Street, against a post chase drawn by Mary Chapman and in which William and John Addington were travelling, whereby the said chase was beat down and overturned and the said William Rhodes did other wrong to William and John Addington.

Verbal abuse generally met with bindovers as the case of John Field, of Leighton Buzzard, who was bound over for threatening to strike John Sanders with a dung drag, and threatening that he would have no more "rest, peace or quietness as long as he lived ."

Minor offences were sometimes punished by the 'Whirligig', a round wooden cage turning on a pivot, the culprit being enclosed and turned with such rapidity that "extreme sickness ensued."

In schools, besides caning and standing in the corner wearing a dunce's cap, there was also the "basket punishment," with a basket which took the form of a wicker cage that was hung from a cross-beam and the child being punished was shut in it, unable to sit down, and was the subject of classmates' "wit."

Punishments were also tough on women and they could be sentenced to "ride the stang" which was a form of ducking stool used to duck the unfortunate victim in the nearest pond.

Drunkards were paraded wearing a tub instead of a cloak with a hole being cut in the bottom for the head to pass through, and two small holes at the sides through which the hands were drawn this was called the drunkard's cloak.

Scolds, or "nagging women" had their heads enclosed in a sugar loaf cap made of iron hooping with a cross at the top and a flat piece of iron projecting inwards that was laid upon the tongue. A string was attached behind the scold who was led through the streets

A widow was successful in getting a relative bound over for threatening to march her to her house and "burn her up in it like a live coal."

There was a clamp down on trading on the Watling Street and traders who placed their goods on the road could be fined, while the fine for placing "corrupt" meat on the highway was 5 shillings.

The arrival of the railways in the 1880's drew trade away from the Watling Street and many pubs had to close because of a decrease in passengers and wagon traffic.

The turnpike trusts that had borrowed money to improve the roads went increasingly into the red, and the Puddlehill Trust which was responsible for the maintenance of the Dunstable-Hockliffe stretch of the Watling Street found its tolls had fallen from £2770 before the railways to £1030 after they started.

The decrease in traffic was so great that grass grew up between the tracks of parts of the Watling Street and there was massive local unemployment which continued until the arrival of the motor car, which gradually improved things.

A great enthusiast for the Watling Street was the celebrated author, Arnold Bennett, who bought a farmhouse in Hockliffe in 1900, and wrote a detective book called, Teresa of Watling Street, which featured many aspects of village life.

He recognised at once the historical associations and the geographical glamour of the Watling Street, its huge length, its extraordinary construction and the drama of the cities and towns that it bisected "like a nerve on its stately progress."

Bennett tracked it diligently on county maps and found it stretched 15 miles south east of Hockliffe, "clothed in its own immortal dust, with scarcely a curve to break the splendid, inexorable monotony of its career."

He wrote: " To me it was a wonderful road - more wonderful than the Great North Road, or the military road from Moscow to Vladivostok. And the most wonderful thing about it was that I lived on it."

Bennett used characters he met in the village in his book, but kept them anonymous. The village of Hockliffe is identified in the first chapter , and is followed by many descriptions of the landscape, including Dunstable, the Chalk Cutting, and the audible chimes of Houghton Regis church.

Reviewing the book, Bedfordshire writer and historian, Simon Houfe said it combines and contrasts the slow pace of rustic life with the whirl of the London financial world - weaving the archetypal villagers of Hockliffe into a gripping tale.

"The book is an amusing read with its moments of romance and undeniable period charm. For the Bedfordshire reader the most engaging passages are those flashes of local colour that are obviously genuinely observed," he wrote.

Just before Arnold Bennett arrived in Hockliffe the first car appeared on the Watling Street. It was a Daimler Phacton which was driven by Mr Dick Ashley, manager of Swansea Corporation, who used it to drive his bride on honeymoon after their marriage at Stony Stratford.

Shortly after this what was believed to be the first fatal accident took place at Shenley when a small boy was run over and killed.

The coroner said at the inquest :" I wonder why there are not more accidents of this kind considering the legislature has allowed what are practically railway engines to run along the roads."

Another crash took place in October, 1908 when a car driven by the Marquis of Northampton was wrecked at Chalk Cutting, Dunstable. The Marquis was unscathed and posed in the wrecked vehicle as if it was a trophy he had just shot.

The crash was greeted with great interest by the local population and a postcard of it was sold in the shops .

One of the earliest drivers was the Rev Capell of Great Brickhill,a local vicar who was said to be a "charming man with a torpedo style beard," and a tiller model de Dion which was his pride and joy." Another driver was a man called "Puffer" Atkinson who had a Mercedes.

The public found the cars extremely noisy, and they particularly disliked the enormous clouds of dust they threw up, and when they came honk-honk-honking along the highway, and there was always rejoicing when one broke down and "faithful old Dobin" was hitched in front to tow it ingloriously home to the blacksmith.

In 1898 the first motor coach in Britain took to the roads round Great Brickhill. It could take 12 passengers, but it did not have a reliable engine, or reliable brakes and it had to be fitted with a "sprag" which was an iron spike which was let down by the conductor when it came to a stop at steep hills, in the hope that it would dig into the roads, and then the passengers would have to get out and push to get the engine started again.

The Watling Street at this time was in a very poor state and full of puddles and mud.

Above: First car on Watling street

A local man commented :"It was one of the busiest thoroughfares in the country, and no other road had so much mechanically propelled traffic, and no one travelled on it unless they had to."

Because of the dust problem, cars were limited to 5 mph in towns and villages, and to help out with the muddy conditions special carts were used, and every house had a mud scraper.

The situation improved in 1905 when it was decided to put tar from the gas works on the road, which brought a new difficulty for horses and livestock in hot weather when the tar got sticky and stuck to their hoofs.

But it did dispose of the dust problem caused by motor vehicles sucking up the dust that came from McAdam new road treatment.

By 1910 all the main roads were tarmacked and the dust and mud problems were greatly alleviated. A survey taken at Stony Stratford in 1910 found that in one week 1,800 horse drawn vehicles, 500 motor cars and 41 traction engines passed through the town.

During the last war there was a big cut down in the amount of traffic using the Watling Street. There was strict petrol rationing and a blackout which caused 3000 deaths, far more than any caused by the Germans.

Headlights were restricted, and had partially covered lights which were stopped from shining upwards, so they would not reveal the whereabouts of the roads to enemy aircraft.

Later traffic increased as convoys of military vehicles made their appearance, and the British had their first look at the American Jeep.

Attacking German bombers used the Watling Street as a position marker and turned left at Redbourn to make for home.

Later when the tide of war turned, British and allied forces also used the Watling Street for the same purpose when they went on bombing raids to Germany.

As far as enemy action was concerned the only incident locally was when a German fighter plane machine gunned the high street of Hockliffe, injuring one person.

The same plane also strafed Dunstable High Street, and shot up the shop windows, but this time there were no casualties, probably because air raid warnings had been given in time, and people had time to take cover in shelters and cellars.

The only other incident appears to have been when a Spitfire crashed just near Dunstable Flying Club and was there for three days while machine gun bullets were removed from it.

But further down The Watling Street at St Albans there was some bomb damage and a few deaths from enemy action and The Watling Street in London suffered severe damage.

In the 1950's the chief problem facing the Watling Street was massive traffic congestion, but when the M1 was opened in 1959 the traffic decreased by half.

But soon the traffic jams came back and a large number of houses that were causing bottle necks were cleared for widening, and among the casualties was the Red Lion pub in Dunstable.

There was quite a lot of antagonism towards the M1 and this has simmered over the years as the jams have got worse. Today it is hard to find the original route of the Watling Street which is buried beneath hardcore, or reconstructed on a parallel site.

Below: Falling by the wayside

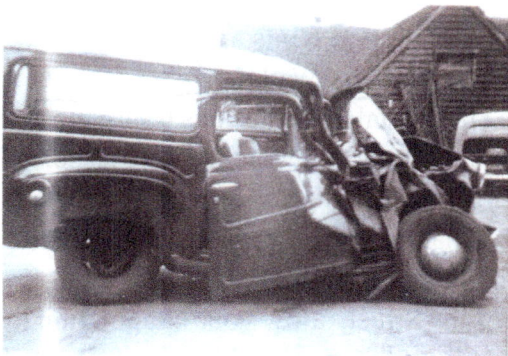

Above: The one that got away

In Staffordshire between the villages and Hints and Weeford close to the western end of the M6 Toll Road the Watling Street is a quiet country road through farmland. This nostalgic route ends traumatically in a vast roundabout from which major roads fan out. Below this noise-ridden island lies the old and forgotten Tolgate crossroads.

Some parts have completely changed but there are still stretches that look very much the same as they were in Roman times.

So when you are in the vicinity of the Street, allow your imagination to take you down to the old road, listen to the sounds of the street, various voices selling their wares, dirty, neglected, tousel-haired waifs. The black-smith kept busy with horses, carts and carriages.

See the stagecoach arriving with tired horses, terrified passangers and strident, bullying coachmen. Hens and mongrel dogs scavange for food. Filthy smelling waste permeates the atmosphere. That's how it was so many years ago.

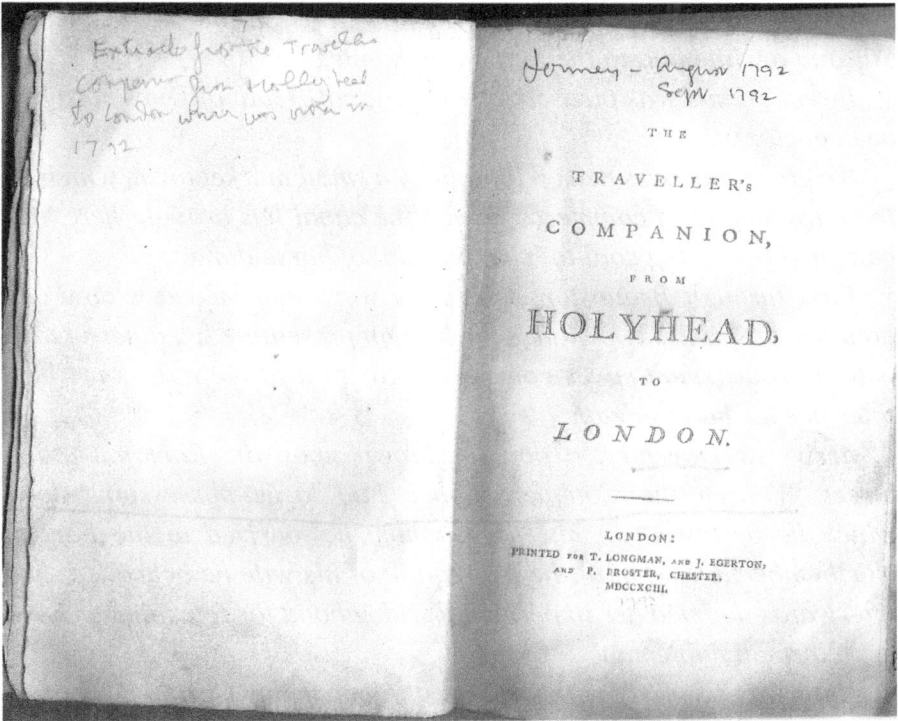

THE TRAVELLER'S COMPANION

FROM HOLYHEAD TO LONDON

1792

Leave Coventry across a common and soon ascend Knighlow Hill, which is one among 40 towns in this hamlet who are obliged to pay Wroth money on every Martinmas Day, in the morning before sunrise; the party paying it, goes three times round the cross and lays the wroth money in a hole before witnesses; the forfeiture for non-observance, is 30s and a white bull to the lord of the hamlet.

I went on and was pleased to see the great Heath of Dunsmore had been enclosed.

We go on and pass near Willoughby, a small market town, which by the introduction of commerce, which the canal has brought here, has benefited by having coal to burn, instead of horse dung.

Pass through Braunston, where we were informed a widow can hold her husband's copy lands for life; on presenting a leathern purse with a groat (small silver coin worth 4d) in it to the next court held after her husband's death.

Arrive at Daventry, a populous town upon the Roman Watling Street. William the Conqueror once had large possessions here, which he bestowed on his niece, whom he married to the Earl of Northumberland who, at the instigation of his wife he beheaded, and afterwards doomed her to perpetual widowhood for refusing her hand to a Norman nobleman.

Here was formerly a Priory, but the imperious Cardinal Woolsey dissolved the house, and appropriated its income to his own college.

Great quantities of whips are manufactured here.

Arrive at Towcester an old market town abounding with good Inns. There was formerly a priory here, while silk stockings and lace are manufactured at this place in great quantities.

On to Whitttlebury Forest, where the trees stretch for nine miles in length with the deep clay being the sort of soil the lusty oak delights on.

There are many deer in the forest, and also wild cats who have been there since the time of Richard I.

The Duke of Grafton is Ranger here and has an elegant mansion called Wakefield Lodge, which was originally built by Mr Claypole the son-in-law of Oliver Cromwell.

Cross the river Ouze and arrive at Stony Stratford, a market town in which the houses are modern, and range on each side of the street.

Edward I erected one of his crosses here, in memory of his Queen Eleanor. A very considerable trade in making bone lace is carried on here.

Pass through Fenny Stratford and ride along a descent of a few miles to Hockley in the hole (Hockliffe) a village that consists almost entirely of inns; near to which stands Battlesden house and park, embellished with woods.

After a few miles ride come to Chalk Hill. There were formerly several gibbets of mail and other robbers, erected here, designed in terrorem to deter men from the commission of such crimes; but by the continuance of the practice of robbing; if every delinquent had been hung in chains, the road might probably have been decorated with gibbets from London to Coventry.

Arrive at Dunstable, a large market town, and was a Roman station, being on the Watling Street road.

Henry 1 to extirpate a gang of robbers, cut down the forests and built a palace here called Kingsbury, (now a farm house).

He likewise with his court, celebrated his Christmas here in 1123 and granted great privileges to the inhabitants. Here was a Priory of Black Cannons at the Reformation, instituted by Henry I.

This town is a great throughfare for travellers and the inns are remarkably elegant.

The uxorious monarch Edward I erected a cross at this place in memory of his Queen Eleanor.

Great numbers of women and children find employment here, in making straw hats, baskets and other articles, in which they show much ingenuity.

The soil is gravelly loam, seemingly very good, and the land fetches about 14 shillings an acre. The Dunstable larks are famous for being the largest and best in the kingdom. Pass through Redburn, where

61

the two martyrs, St Alban and St Amphybalus are said to have been interred. Here the soil abounds with flinty stones; the improvements made use by the farmers is chalk, which endures for many years, without being renewed.

Gorhambury, formerly belonging to the abbey of St Albans, and afterwards the paternal estate of the great Sir Francis Bacon, Lord Verulam, stands at a short distance; it is an ancient grand structure, including some very magnificent rooms which are embellished with a most capital collection of portraits of great personages; it is now the seat of Lord Grimstone.

Soon reach the ancient Verulamium which was a stronghold of the Britons before the invasion of Julius Caesar, and being the capital of the country, was at that time the residents of its princes, and had its mint, for coining money.

The great fragments of thick walls are evidence of it, having been a Roman city, and by them fortified in the strongest manner.

The walls encircled the city, they were formed of layers of flints and mortar with courses, or tiers of brick, interlaid at distances of between two and three feet. The Roman bricks were not always made uniform in size.

Verulanium together with some other cities was sacked by the furious Boadicea; who put upwards of 70 thousand persons to death for their attachment to the religion and customs of the Romans.

Here were formerly subterraneous, passages and vaults, intended for places of retreat, and security in time of war.

St Albans town arose from the ruins of Verulamium, and took its name from Alban, the first English martyr, who suffered under the persecution of Diocletian.

Offa, King of the Mercians erected a very fine monastery here, and endowed it with great revenue. It was formerly the residence of the Saxon Princes and Mitred Abbots.

There are no vestiges of this once magnificent Abbey remaining now, except for the gateway. The murderous hand of time has removed a structure, which once held the bones of the famous Martyr, enclosed in a golden shrine.

It was the great resort of pilgrims, and was possessed of a vast revenue, and great riches, which if they had been applied to the repairs of the building, might have continued its splendour, even to this time, but the reforming spirit of Henry VIII, dissolved this, with other religious houses in 1538.

The ancient Abbots, are said to have dined in a great hall, seated on an elevated part, and to have been served on plate by the monks; other religious guests placing themselves at the tables along the sides of the hall.

The present church is very ancient and is ornamented with a fine tower, upwards of 140 ft high. It seems to have been built, or repaired at different times.

The choir is in the Gothic style, embellished with fine old tabernacle work. The high altar is a beautiful specimen of Gothic sculpture; in the niches, were formerly placed images of gold and silver. A small gallery remains, in which a monk was used to keep continual watch over these valuable treasures.

Here are several very magnificent tombs, amongst which are those of King Offa, St Alban, Humphry Duke of Gloucester, and Abbot Ramridge; there are other monuments of mitred abbots, and warriors, worthy the notice of the curious traveller.

It is governed by a Mayor, recorder, 12 aldermen and 24 assistants. The town was formerly fortified, and was the scene of horrid slaughter, both in the Baron's wars, as likewise in the civil wars between the Houses of York and Lancaster.

The two famous battles fought here, stand distinguished in the history of those dreadful times.

Now we go on and pass through London Colney, and come to Wrotham Park an elegant house built by the unfortunate Admiral John

Byng, who though acquitted of cowardice was shot for an error in judgement.

But it is thought now, that if some other persons had been executed for the failure of that expedition; that their sentence would have born a more malignant term. than that, to which the poor Admiral fell a sacrifice.

In a short ride reach Barnet, where there is a famous market for swine, and other cattle. The church is ancient; and here are alms houses, and other charitable institutions.

On Barnet Common a column is erected to commemorate the battle that was fought here between the Yorkists and Lancastrians, on the 4th of April, 1471, when the King maker, Warwick, was totally defeated and slain, and Edward IV restored to his throne.

The conflict lasted from four o'clock in the morning, until ten at night, and Edward VII restores to his throne.

The pleasant village of Hadley is at a small distance. The church is built of flintstones. Over the door is the date 1498 and on the steeple there is yet to be seen, an iron pitch-pot which was formerly to be set on fire, for the purpose of alarming the country in troublesome times, or upon an invasion. These sort of beacons were first directed by King Edward III.

The village is upon the outskirts of Enfield Chase, which continued to be a large forest, till the year 1778, when it was enclosed, and measured 8,394 acres.

Pass over the extensive Common of Finchley which the traveller a few years ago crossed in fear, apprehending a visit from the numerous gangs of highwaymen, that infested this road.

The Mail Coaches, which now are passing at all hours, have a guard, always properly armed, and this may account for the less frequency of robberies in these parts.

Highgate now presents itself on an eminence which overlooks the whole Metropolis.

A toll gate was set-up here, more than 400 years ago, by the Bishop of London, which was afterwards farmed by Queen Elizabeth at 40l a year.

Some of the public houses have a large pair of horns placed over the sign, and when any travellers stop for refreshment, the horns are produced, and are pressingly solicited to be sworn.

If they consent a burlesque kind of oath is administered, that they will never eat brown bread when they can get white, and several other declarations of the like which they repeat with one hand placed upon the horns.

If a female is sworn, she has a privilege to say "except I like the other better."

The ceremony being over, they kiss the horns, and pay one shilling to be spent by the company. In a short ride of five miles we reach the metropolis.   FINIS.

The Highwayman

By Alfred Noyes

*The wind was a torrent of darkness among the gusty
trees,
The moon was a ghostly galleon tossed upon
cloudy seas,
The road was a ribbon of moonlight over the
purple moor,
And the highwayman came riding - Riding-riding
The Highwayman came riding up to the old
inn-door.*

*He'd a French cocked-hat on his forehead, a bunch
of lace on his chin,
A coat of the claret velvet, and breeches of brown
doe-skin;
They fitted with never a wrinkle; his boots were up
to the thigh!
And he rode with a jewelled twinkle,
His pistol butts a-twinkle,
His rapier hilt a twinkle under the jewelled
sky,
Over the cobbles he clattered and clashed in
the dark inn-yard,
And he tapped with his whip on the shutters, but all
was locked and barred;
He whistled a tune to the window, and who should
be waiting there*

But the landlord's black-eyed daughter,
Bess, the landlord's daughter,
The landlord's red-lipped daughter
Plaiting a dark red love knot into her
long black hair.

And dark in the dark old inn-yard a
stable- wicket creaked
Where Tim the ostler listened; his face was
white and peaked;
His eyes were hollows of madness, his hair
like mouldy hay,
But he loved the landlord's daughter,
The landlord's red-lipped daughter,
Dumb as a dog he listened, and he heard the
robber say-
" One kiss my bonny sweetheart, I'm after
a prize tonight,
But I shall be back with the yellow gold before
the morning night;
Yet, if they press me sharply, and harry me
through the day,
Then look for me by moonlight,
Watch for me by moonlight,
I'll come to thee by moonlight, though
hell shall bar the way."

He rose upright in the stirrups; he scarce
could reach her hand,
But she loosened her hair i' the casement!
His face burnt like a brand
And the black cascade of perfume came

tumbling over his breast;
And he kissed his waves in the moonlight
(Oh sweet black waves in the moonlight!)
Then he tugged at his rein in the moonlight,
and galloped away to the West.

He did not come in the dawning; he did not
come at noon;
And out o' the tawny sunset, before the rise o'
the moon.
When the road was a gipsy's ribbon, looping
the purple moor,
A red-coat troop came marching
Marching-marching-
King George's men came marching up to the
old inn door.

They said no word to the landlord, they drank
his ale instead,
But they gagged his daughter and bound her to
the foot of her narrow bed;
Two of them knelt at her casement, with
muskets at their side!
There was death at every window;
And hell at one dark window;
For Bess could see through her casement,
the road that he would ride.

They had tied her up to attention, with many a
a sniggering jest;
They had bound a musket beside her, with the
barrel beneath her breast!

"Now keep good watch!" and they kissed her.
they kissed her.
She heard the dead man say - Look for me
by moonlight!
Watch for me by moonlight!
I'll come to thee by moonlight though hell
should bar the way!

She twisted her hands behind her; but all the knots held good
She writhed her hands till her fingers were wet
with sweat or blood!
They stretched and strained in the darkness, and
the hours crawled by like years.
Till now on the stroke of midnight,
The tip of her finger touched it!
The trigger at least was hers!

The tip of one finger touched it; she strove no more for
the rest!
Up she stood up to attention, with the barrel
beneath her breast,
She would not risk their hearing; she would not
strive again!
For the road lay bare in the moonlight;
Blank and bare in the moonlight;
And the blood of her veins in the moonlight throbbed
to her love's refrain.

Tlot-tlot;tlot, tlot! Had they heard it? The horse-hoofs
ringing clear;
Tlot-tlot, tlot-tlot in the distance ? Where they deaf
that they did not hear?

*Down the ribbon of moonlight, over the brow
of the hill,
The highwayman came riding,
Riding, riding!
The red-coats looked to their priming! She stood
up straight and still!*

*Tlot, tlot in the frosty silence! Tlot, tlot in the echoing
  night!
Nearer he came and nearer! Her face was like a light!
Her eyes grew wide for a moment, she drew one last
deep breath,
Then her finger moved in the moonlight,
Her musket shattered the moonlight,
Shattered her breast in the moonlight
and warned him - with her death.*

*He turned; he spurred to the Westward, he did not
  know who stood
Bowed with her head over the musket, drenched with
her own red blood!
Not till the dawn he heard it, and his face grew grey
to hear
How Bess the landlord's daughter,
The landlord's black-eyed daughter,
Had watched for her love in the moonlight , and died
in the darkness there.
Back he spurred like madman, shrieking a curse to the
sky,
With the white road smoking behind him and his
rapier brandished high!
Blood red were his spurs i, the golden noon;*

wine red was his velvet coat;
When they shot him down on the highway,
Down like a dog on the highway,
As he lay in his blood on the highway; with the bunch
of lace at his throat.

And still of a winters night they say, when the wind is
in the trees,
When the moon is a ghastly galleon tossed upon
cloudy seas,
When the road is a ribbon of moonlight over the
purple moor,
A highwayman comes riding -
Riding-riding-
A highwayman comes riding, up to the old inn-door.

Over the cobbles he clatters and clangs in the dark
inn-yard;
And he taps with his whip on the shutters, but all
is locked and barred;
He whistles a tune to the window, and who should
be waiting there,
But the landlord's black-eyed daughter,
Bess , the landlord's daughter,
Plaiting a dark red love-knot into her long
black hair.

APPENDIX

Roman Verulanmum. Guide Book, Verulamium Museum
Historic Hertfordshire, W.P Westell
Old Hertfordshire Calendar, D.J. Baker
Short History of the English People, J.R.Green
Hockliffe, Beds Parish Survey, S.R. Coleman
History of Bedfordshire, Joyce Godber, Bedfordshire County Council.
Kelly's Directory of Bedfordshire 1928
Post Office Directory of Hertfordshire 1878
History of Dunstable, W.H. Derbyshire
Bedfordshire County Records 1714-1832
Bedfordshire and Huntingdonshire Early History of England
The Story of St Albans, E. Toms
Highways and Byways of Hertfordshire, H.W. Tompkins
Hertfordshire, H.W. Tompkins
The Bedfordshire and Huntingdonshire Landscape, P. Bigmore
Dunstable. Its History and Surroundings, Worthington Smith
Barmy Bedfordshire, R.W. Dawson
The Lost Villages of Bedfordshire, R.W. Dawson

The Watling Street being repaired at The Square, Hockliffe

CPSIA information can be obtained at www.ICGtesting.com
Printed in the USA
BVOW11s2344100914

366267BV00005BA/11/P